THINGS THAT STING

Hornets

By Amy Hayes

Gareth Stevens PUBLISHING

Please visit our website, www.garethstevens.com. For a free color catalog of all our high-quality books, call toll free 1-800-542-2595 or fax 1-877-542-2596.

Library of Congress Cataloging-in-Publication Data

Hayes, Amy.
Hornets / Amy Hayes.
pages cm. — (Things that sting)
Includes index.
ISBN 978-1-4824-1699-2 (pbk.)
ISBN 978-1-4824-1700-5 (6 pack)
ISBN 978-1-4824-1698-5 (library binding)
1. Hornets—Juvenile literature. I. Title.
QL568.V5H39 2014
595.79'8—dc23

2014021956

First Edition

Published in 2016 by
Gareth Stevens Publishing
111 East 14th Street, Suite 349
New York, NY 10003

Designer: Nicholas Domiano
Editor: Kristen Rajczak

Photo credits: Cover, p. 1 Christian Schoissingeyer/Shutterstock.com; title texture: Asya Alexandrova/Shutterstock.com; caption box: VectorShots/Shutterstock.com; p. 5 Bezuglaya Tatiana/Shutterstock.com; p. 7 © iStockphoto/RoseMaryBush; p. 9 Nancy Bauer/Shutterstock.com; p. 11 © iStockphoto/RolfAasa; p. 13 © iStockphoto/SHSPhotography; p. 15 (main) © Trancelius/Wikimedia Commons; p. 15 (inset) © iStockphoto/contrail1; p. 17 Shin.T/Moment/Getty Images; p. 19 © iStockphoto/showcake; p. 21 Dennis van de Water/Shutterstock.com.

Printed in the United States of America

CPSIA compliance information: Batch #CS16GS: For further information contact Gareth Stevens, New York, New York at 1-800-542-2595.

Contents

Words in the glossary appear in **bold** type the first time they are used in the text.

Where in the World Are Hornets?

Hornets are some of the most amazing, fearless creatures on the planet. Their ability to sting means they're some of the deadliest, too.

There are about 20 different species, or kinds, of hornets. Most of them live in Asia. The hornets you might see in your backyard are European hornets people likely brought to North America. These hornets were first spotted in New York in 1840, and they've been here ever since. Today, they're found in much of the United States.

The European hornet is the only kind of true hornet found in North America.

Parts and Pieces

Hornets are insects, which means their body is divided into three parts: head, **thorax**, and **abdomen**. The hornet has a sharp stinger at the end of its abdomen. It also has six legs with razor-sharp edges that make them perfect for attacking other insects.

With their black and yellow stripes and four wings, hornets look very similar to **wasps** and yellow jackets. This is because they're very closely related. Hornets and yellow jackets are actually types of wasps.

THAT SMARTS!

Hornets use their sharp legs as spears to fight other bugs. Hornets take on bees, spiders, and even praying mantises!

Hornets are fierce fighters and will take on any enemy.

What Does a Hornet Call Home?

Hornets live in big colonies called hives. They make the hive by chewing up wood until it forms a pulp, which looks somewhat like wet paper. This pulp is a light but strong material for the hornets. Once the hornets have the pulp they need, they build by spreading it with their legs.

When the hornets are finished, the hive looks like a big, upside-down teardrop. The hornets enter and exit through the tip of the teardrop, right at the bottom of the hive.

THAT SMARTS!

It's very dangerous to try to get rid of a hornets' nest. ***Exterminators*** *wear full* ***protective*** *suits sealed at the wrists to prevent any angry hornets from stinging them!*

Hornets like to build their nests out of the way, such as hidden high in trees.

Members of the Hive

The first member of a colony is the queen. There is only one queen per nest. She is the largest hornet and the only one who can lay eggs. In the fall, future queens hatch and **mate** with male hornets. These queens each spend the winter hiding from the cold.

In the spring, new queens build small nests and lay their first eggs. Some of these young grow to be worker females who can't lay eggs. They add on to the nest and do other work around the hive.

That Smarts!

Most hornets are female. Any hornets you see flying around certainly are. That's because male hornets never leave the hive. Their only job is to mate with the queen hornet.

Queens lay between 1,000 and 2,000 eggs total.

A Hornet's Upbringing

Hornet eggs are small and white. After a time, they grow into **larvae** and then **pupae**. Worker hornets bring food to each pupa as it grows. During the pupa stage, the hornet is a **carnivore**. For food, worker hornets hunt other insects and feed them to the pupae.

Some adult hornets will attack beehives to eat the bees and their young. But adult hornets aren't just carnivores. They eat honey and tree sap as well as other insects.

That Smarts!

Hunting for food for the pupae can be tiring, but hornets have a special trick. When a hornet feeds a pupa, the pupa creates ***saliva*** *that gives a huge energy boost to the adult hornets. It's like a strong cup of coffee!*

Hornets can fly up to 60 miles (96.5 km) a day when they drink pupa saliva!

Protecting the Nest

Once a hornet has grown up, it has about 4 weeks to live. Hornets have lots of jobs, but the most important one is protecting the hive. To do that, hornets do what they do best. They sting!

Hornets are one of the most dreaded stinging creatures in the world. Unlike some other stinging insects, such as bees, hornets can sting many times. A hornet's stinger is sharp and smooth, so that it can pierce the skin and come back out again.

That Smarts!

Hornets don't just sting—they bite! They have mouthparts called mandibles that can deliver a painful chomp.

Hornets don't usually attack people unless the people get too close to their nest. If you see a hornet's nest, stay far away.

Big, Bad Hornets

When people think of deadly hornets, they're usually talking about the Asian giant hornet. Of all the hornet species, it's the biggest and most dangerous.

Living in Southeast Asia, China, and Japan, the giant hornet isn't something you'll have to worry about in your backyard. That's lucky, because Asian giant hornets are about 2 inches (5 cm) long, and have a stinger that's about 1/4 inch (6 mm) long. An Asian giant hornet can grow bigger than your thumb!

THAT SMARTS!

There's a sports drink in Japan called VAAM that has matter from Asian giant hornets in it!

The scientific name for the Asian giant hornet is *Vespa mandarinia*.

Dangerous Stings

Hornet stings can be dangerous for a lot of reasons. Many people are **allergic** to hornet stings, and they can get very sick if a hornet stings them.

The other problem is that it's unlikely to be stung just once. Hornets not only sting multiple times, but also may **swarm** and attack in a group. Some hornet stings are poisonous, too. If a person gets stung enough times, that poison can cause serious damage, like kidney failure.

THAT SMARTS!

If you find yourself close to a swarm of hornets, try to stay calm. Walk away slowly and quietly.

Hornet stings are painful and can be deadly.

Hornets in Our World

Hornets are amazing creatures, but many people worry about the dangers of having them close by. Hornets have moved into neighborhoods in China, making their nests on the sides of buildings and attacking people who get too close. Many people are worried about upsetting a hornets' nest, and lots of exterminators have been called.

However, hornets are an important part of nature. In fact, certain countries, including Germany, protect hornets to make sure they will be making nests long into the future.

That Smarts!

Low hornet populations in Germany were caused by people fearing hornets and then killing too many of them.

A Hornet's Body

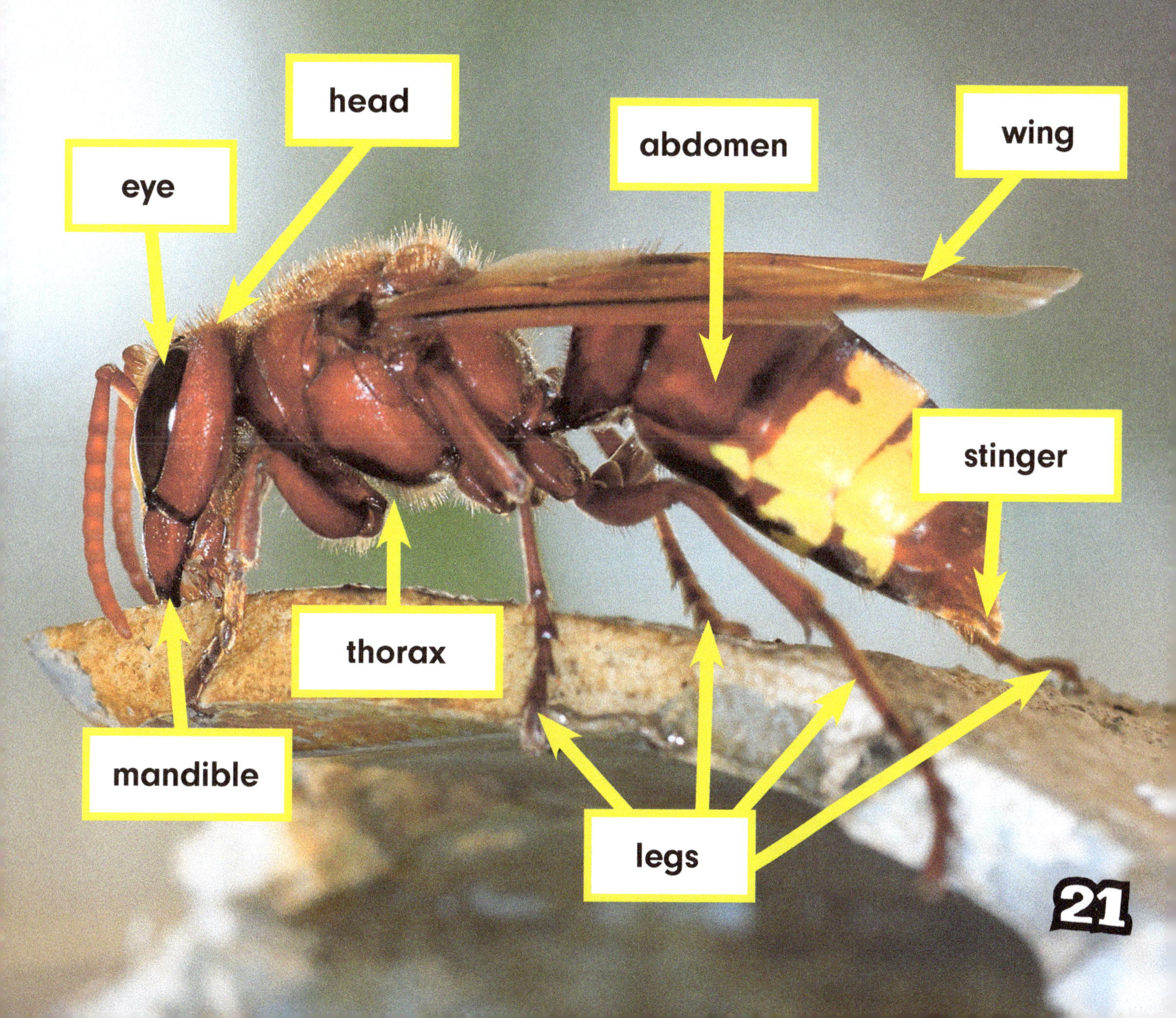

Glossary

abdomen: the part of an insect's body that contains the stomach

allergic: to have a sensitivity to usually harmless things in the surroundings, such as dust, pollen, or insect stings

carnivore: an animal that eats only meat

exterminator: someone who gets rid of pests

larvae: bugs in an early life stage that have a wormlike form. The singular form is "larva."

mate: to come together to produce babies

protective: keeping safe

pupae: bugs that are changing from larvae to adults. The singular form is "pupa."

saliva: a watery matter animals make in their mouth to help break down food

swarm: to move somewhere in large numbers. Also, a group of insects.

thorax: the section of an insect's body that contains the heart and lungs. In hornets, the legs and wings are attached to the thorax.

wasp: any of numerous winged insects related to bees and ants that have a slender body with the abdomen attached by a narrow stalk

For More Information

Books

Markle, Sandra. *Hornets: Incredible Insect Architects*. Minneapolis, MN: Lerner Publications Company, 2008.

Pallotta, Jerry. *Hornet vs. Wasp*. New York, NY: Scholastic, 2013.

Websites

Asian Giant Hornet
a-z-animals.com/animals/asian-giant-hornet/
Find out exciting facts about the scariest hornet species.

Hornets
animals.nationalgeographic.com/animals/bugs/hornet/
Check out the life cycle of the hornet and some really cool videos, too!

Publisher's note to educators and parents: Our editors have carefully reviewed these websites to ensure that they are suitable for students. Many websites change frequently, however, and we cannot guarantee that a site's future contents will continue to meet our high standards of quality and educational value. Be advised that students should be closely supervised whenever they access the Internet.

Index